How to Get Paid Before Going Pro

Before Going Pro

The Parent Guide to NIL

By

Joy Harris

How to Get Paid Before Going Pro
The Parent Guide to NIL

ISBN 978-0-9985167-4-5

Score
3420 Pump Road
No. 279
Henrico, VA 23233

First Edition

Designed by Joy Harris and Sydney Harris

Illustrations and Interior Layout by Joy Harris

DISCLAIMER

The content provided in this book is designed to provide helpful information on the subjects discussed. This book is not meant to be used, nor should it be used, to diagnose or treat any medical condition. The numbers in this book are theoretical and to be used for illustrative purposes only. The publisher and the author are not responsible for any actions you take or do not take as a result of reading this book and are not liable for any damages or negative consequences from action or inaction to any person reading or following the information in this book. References are provided for informational purposes only and do not constitute endorsement of any people, websites or other sources.

Readers should also be aware that the websites listed in this book may change or become obsolete.

Thank You

To Ryan and Sydney for teaching me myself

To Demond for the push to write this book and cheering

me on

"Ones up"

CONTENTS

INTRODUCTION

One hot Saturday afternoon during the car ride home after my son's disappointing rec football loss, I was gazing out the window, trying to recover from the blaze of the sun, when my son uttered words that would stop me in my tracks. "Mom, Dad. I want to play football."

I half-way listened, still too hot to have a bunch of banter fill the car.

"Okay," my husband said.

My son, sensing his point hadn't come across, tried again. "I mean, when I grow up. I want to play football."

Immediately, every flashing red, "do not pass go, do not collect $200.00" sign in my head went off. As the co-owner of a million dollar service company, I couldn't wrap my head around the decision. Discipline, exercise, and competition were one thing. But it's a totally different thing to put your body at risk without being paid until you graduate college and go pro, where the average run is only three years of play.

I just couldn't see sending him to a gauntlet with a 1% chance of success, a fate he couldn't control, and ZERO chance of income for YEARS, only to make an average of $85,390* for three years after that. Yes, contrary to the big headlines, the average professional athlete across all sports makes approximately $85,390, and the average career of a NFL player is three years. Don't get me wrong, $85,390 is more money than most make in a year, but when you compare that to the annual salary the average successful entrepreneur or high-level manager makes from a corporate gig (and the fact that they can do their job for longer with less bodily harm) it was a bad idea to me with a capital B.

"Are you sure you don't want to play badminton or do something easier that's indoors?" I said, trying to throw the idea off with a joke. "You know you can make more money working for me than playing pro football, and you can make it sooner—or even land a six-figure career in less time with less impact on your body."

Side note: for the record, I'm a mama bear, more like the bear in the movie *The Revenant* when she thought her cubs were going to be harmed by Leonardo DiCaprio than an overbearing mother. This means the grueling trek to pro football, where they cycle you through until your body cannot yield gladiator results and then dispose of you, was definitely not on the list of my options for my kid.

But he said he wanted to play, and as his parent, one thing I'm committed to above my own desires is to support him in his. So with that in mind, I agreed, and I began my hunt for a window of opportunity like I'd do for any other business in a tough market. While compiling his strategy, we capitalized on the thing that I hope has brought you to this book: NIL.

The goal of this book is to show you how you can use NIL to build a financial nest egg your student-athlete can use to either graduate from college debt-free or set up the next chapter of their life. I'll be walking you through how to build this nest egg, but these are all steps you can teach your athlete and encourage them to take the responsibility for. I've helped 107 parents and student athletes enter the world of NIL, grow their personal brand, and generate income. Now I want to help you and your athlete succeed in the world of NIL too.

*Occupational Outlook Handbook, Us Bureau of Labor Statistics, 2021, bls.gov

1 UNDERSTANDING THE NAME, IMAGE AND LIKENESS LANDSCAPE

Welcome to the exciting world of Name, Image, and Likeness (NIL). In this chapter, we'll explore the hot concept that has transformed the landscape of college athletics. Get ready to dive deep into the realm of empowerment, opportunity, and uncharted possibilities as I unravel the enigma that is NIL.

Empowering the Athletes

NIL represents a seismic shift in the way college athletes are perceived–and the way they perceive themselves. No longer at the mercy of being chosen by a coach, school, or team before their hard works yields the ability to take care of their life off the field, these talented individuals can now harness the power of their name, image, and personal brand to create the type of success they want for their life right now. With the ability to monetize their skills and influence, student-athletes are empowered like never before, becoming architects of their own destiny and shattering the glass ceiling of collegiate limitations.

A student-athlete can now earn money by endorsing products, starring in commercials, and launching their own business. It's like a real-life episode of *The Price Is Right*, where the only question is, "How much is your autograph worth?" Suddenly, every student-athlete (including yours) has the potential to be a walking, talking billboard.

Contrary to what you might have heard, NIL is not just for five-star athletes. It's not exclusive to D1 athletes. It's definitely not limited to athletes who have millions of followers. NIL is for *your* athlete, and the rest of this book aims to show you how to use it to their advantage.

Unlocking the Entrepreneurial Spirit

The advent of NIL has opened up a treasure trove of opportunities for student-athletes. Gone are the days of struggling to make ends meet while pursuing their passions. Now, athletes can leverage their popularity to secure endorsement deals, sponsorships, and lucrative partnerships. Picture a linebacker sitting in front of a vanity mirror, practicing their best smize (smiling with their eyes) for a high-end cosmetics company. Or a soccer player posing as a fashionista, strutting down the runway in a couture gown made entirely of recycled sports equipment. Athletes are discovering their hidden talents and passions, transforming themselves into multi-faceted individuals. From apparel collaborations and social media campaigns to hosting events, giving motivational speeches, and launching fitness apps, the avenues for financial growth and professional development are boundless.

Building Lifelong Skills

Beyond the monetary benefits, NIL equips student-athletes with invaluable life skills that transcend the sports arena. From negotiating contracts and managing finances to building a personal brand and engaging with their fan base, athletes are gaining real-world experience that will serve them well in their future endeavors. NIL encourages them to become astute communicators, savvy marketers, responsible money managers, and socially conscious individuals who understand the power of their platform.

The Origin

To understand the gravity of NIL and its undeniable transformation to the student-athlete landscape, you must first understand its origin.

For decades, the NCAA maintained a strict policy that prohibited college athletes from profiting off their own names, images, and likenesses. The use of this right was reserved only for the NCAA, which they used as leverage for media distribution. For example, in 2010, the NCAA signed a 14-year media deal with CBS for $10 billion, then extended this agreement in 2023 for $900,000 each year.

However, winds of change began to blow, and the clamor for justice grew louder. In 2009 the NCAA lost the O'Bannon case, which meant the NCAA could not prohibit its member schools from allowing student-athlete scholarships or education-related payments up to the full cost of tuition. The antitrust class action law suite paved the way for what is now NIL. And in

2021, the NCAA adopted a uniform interim policy suspending NCAA name, image and likeness rules for all incoming and current student-athletes in all sports, heralding a new era of empowerment and autonomy for athletes.

The policy provides the following guidance to college athletes, recruits, their families, and member schools:

- Individuals can engage in NIL activities that are consistent with the law of the state where the school is located. Colleges and universities may be a resource for state law questions.

- College athletes who attend a school in a state without an NIL law can engage in this type of activity without violating NCAA rules related to name, image, and likeness.

- Individuals can use a professional services provider for NIL activities.

- Student-athletes should report NIL activities consistent with state law or school and conference requirements to their school.

One of the most significant benefits of pursuing NIL is the newfound financial empowerment it brings. Student-athletes, previously restricted from monetizing their own skills and popularity, can now unlock a world of revenue streams. Through endorsement deals, merchandise sales, and sponsored collaborations, athletes have the chance to generate income that can alleviate financial burdens, support their education, and lay a foundation for a prosperous future, whether or not they go pro.

NIL offers college athletes an unprecedented platform to build and cultivate their personal brand. By effectively leveraging their unique skills, personalities, and stories, athletes can connect with a broader audience, both on and off the field. Texas basketball player Shaylee Gonzales had the opportunity to do just that when NIL allowed her to expand into fashion and become the face of a company obsessed with vintage clothing. Through social media, content creation, and community engagement, athletes can shape their public image and establish a lasting legacy that extends far beyond their collegiate years. This can also position your athlete in front of the executives of companies that can offer them future careers (executives they would not have connected with previously).

Pursuing NIL opportunities also provides invaluable professional development for college athletes. By engaging in contract negotiations, managing endorsements, and collaborating with companies, athletes gain firsthand experience in the business world. These experiences cultivate essential skills such as communication, negotiation, and relationship building, which can serve them well in their future careers, whether those careers are in sports or another field. And the financial leverage can even be a launchpad for entrepreneurship.

NIL allows athletes to amplify their voices and make a lasting impact on social and cultural issues. By leveraging their platform, athletes can champion causes close to their hearts, raise awareness about important social issues, and inspire change. (Quarterback Nick Evans at the University of Wisconsin uses the money he earns from meet-and-greets and autograph signings to support the Make-A-Wish Foundation.) They become influential figures, using their popularity to drive meaningful conversations, create charitable initiatives, and advocate for positive societal transformations.

2 BUILDING A PERSONAL BRAND

Now that you know what NIL is, let's talk about how
you can access the opportunity for your athlete.
Student-athletes inherently have fans, followers, and an
audience rooting for them on a regular basis just
because of their athletic performance. Because of this,
companies know athletes are the perfect way to get
their services and products in front of their target
audiences. This attention partnership is common at the
professional level. Think Michael Jordan and Nike or
Serena Williams and Beats by Dre. Now these
companies can finally work with student-athletes.

The good news is that your athlete does not have to
have a mega-following like Serena Williams. What your
athlete does need is engagement. Engagement is a
fancy way of saying your athlete needs a group of

people that actually interact with them and stick with them on a regular basis. It has been shown that athletic influencers tend to have a higher engagement rate than an average influencer (12% vs 4%), which makes athletic influencers a no-brainer for companies to work with. To cultivate this engagement, your athlete needs a personal brand.

Your athlete possesses a unique combination of talents, dedication, and determination. These traits are the basis of what it takes to build a personal brand. By understanding your athlete's interests and strengths, you can help them define their identity and create an authentic and compelling brand that resonates with fans, sponsors, and their future audience.

Personal Brand Explained

A Personal brand is a way to identify yourself as different from others.

For example, if you look at the two photos below, the only noticeable difference between the two shirts is the symbol. In the case of the shirts, the company branding conveys the type of person that might wear the product (fashionista versus athlete), what they might value (style versus function), and what partnerships the company might participate in. Your athlete's personal brand does the same thing. It identifies their audience, what they're into, and who should rock with them.

Who can build a personal brand? Everyone. No matter your athlete's social media presence, athletic record, or grade level, your athlete can build a personal brand.

How to Create a Personal Brand

Now, for the question I get a lot. What should my athlete's brand be? Because a brand is all about being unique, it's important that the brand be authentic to your athlete. Sure, there may be popular trends or a certain way a big-time YouTuber does things, but remember that brand is already taken. It would be like taking the Nike Swoosh off of your athlete's slides, pasting it onto a hoodie you buy from Target, and saying you have a new clothing line. People aren't going to see it as something valuable, but rather as just a copy of a better original product. They will almost always choose to stay loyal to the original and won't stick with you.

To figure out what your brand should be, let's use the *AND Formula.*

Personal Brand = <u>Sport</u> + <u>Actual Interest</u>

The first blank is easy. It's the sport your athlete currently plays. The second answer should be what your athlete does the majority of the time when they are not playing their sport. It can be playing video games, testing home remedies for allergies, photography, or chewing different types of gum. There are no wrong answers here. The only rule is your athlete MUST be into it. Like REALLY into it. Like they talk about it so much that you've learned to say "yeah, uh-huh" to them without actually listening. That thing that seems boring, weird or normal. That is the second part of the formula. If your athlete's recurring activity popped in your head and you immediately thought, "That can't be it," that IS the correct answer.

> **Tip**: *Don't know where to start? Have your athlete scroll their social media feed and tell you the content they watch the most. The answer is in there.*

Now complete the formula below:

My athlete plays _____ and _____.

You know what your athlete's brand is, but where should you use it so companies who want to pay for their endorsement will see it? Everywhere! More specifically, everywhere your athlete's audience is. But let's take it one step at a time.

Right now, there's one platform your athlete is on more than the others. As I'm writing this, it's probably TikTok, YouTube, or Snapchat. But it could also be newer platforms like Twitch or Threads, so don't assume. Ask them.

For the sake of the example, let's say your athlete is on TikTok all the time. You're going to want TikTok to be the jumping-off point. That platform is where you're going to assist them in making as much content as possible. Then, you're going to look at that content the following day, take the pieces that do the best in views and engagement, and repurpose them on all of your athlete's other platforms. Repurposing content is when you take a post that's already on your athlete's social media page and tweak it a bit to make it fresh and new. For example, this tweak might mean adding captions, graphics, or music.

> **Tip**: You can go in your account settings on most social media platforms and add your athlete's account. That way you can easily access their account for posting.

If step one is identifying your athlete's personal brand and step two is learning where to post, step three is figuring out *what* to post. Posting something consistently on social media can feel a bit awkward or intimidating. To keep this simple, I break it down into "cars" and "lanes."

There are three content "cars": video, audio and written word. On social media, you can either record a video, record your voice, or write. Some platforms combine these forms, such as Instagram incorporating video Reels and written captions, but for now, let's keep the three categories separate. The important part is talking to your athlete about the three content options so you can determine the most natural "car" for them.

It's true that video is king right now, but if your athlete is not comfortable being on camera, it doesn't mean all hope is lost. You might just need to use a little creativity. If they're really good at writing, put most of their content on a platform like Medium where they can write articles and stories about their interests. Then you can take those words, insert them on top of a photo in your phone, and let TikTok's voice animation feature read their words to their audience. Once you post it, it becomes a video that can then be repurposed again for Instagram by making it a Reel and adding a caption. There you have three pieces of content without your athlete ever being on camera.

If your athlete loves talking but not being on camera, use your phone to create a podcast. You can also text them questions and have them send you voice memos of the answers that you combine into a podcast episode.

If they're fine with being on camera, remember, what they do does not have to be like anyone else. Khabe Lame created a personal brand that generates over $4 million per year without ever saying a word. Your athlete can do skits, draw pictures, or give tutorials. The sky's the limit.

If the "car" is how you create content, the "lane" is what you create to get in front of companies. Going back to your *AND Formula*, the lanes are the categories within the interest you have.

There are four "lanes": news, technical, art, and humor. I have included examples below, but the possibilities are endless.

Content Lanes

News	Fun Facts, What's Happening in the Industry, Reviews
Technical	Gadgets, How To Tips, Breakdowns
Art	Visual Art, Music, Making Things
Humor	Skits, Reactions, Commentary

Your athlete can mix and match "lanes". You can even incorporate trends, behind-the-scenes, or day-in-the-life content as icing on the cake. The most important part is that you post.

To begin creating, don't run out and buy any equipment. You probably already have a corner full of sports equipment piled up somewhere. Let's save ourselves the same headache here. Start with your phone and your athlete's phone and a free video editing app like CapCut or InShot.

Remember to let your athlete embrace their unique experiences, perspectives, and challenges, because those shape their identity. They can even share their daily growth, challenges, and mistakes as they dive deeper into their interest. These stories connect them more to their audience on a personal level, showcasing their authenticity and inspiring others along the way.

Authenticity is the cornerstone of a strong personal brand. This isn't time for the media-trained version of your athlete that appears for the press after a bad game. This is the opportunity for their true self to shine through. Avoid the temptation to portray them as polished or conform to others' expectations.

Let's recap: You have your personal brand. You know the platform to dump most of your content on. You know what content to post based on your athlete's "car" and "lanes".

> **Tip**: *Have your athlete clean up social media. Be authentic, just keep in mind, a brand wants customers to purchase their product. That means the less friction between the customer and their product, the better. If people come to your page and are immediately turned off because of products or activities you have on your page, you may want to change it. You don't have to please or appeal to everyone, but you should be mindful of how to win the game you want to play in.*

Now let's put it all together. Yes, your athlete can continue posting training, practices and game highlights, but now they're also going to post content about their brand.

Look at your athlete's schedule and see where there are opportunities for them to create as much content as possible. Set a reminder in the calendar on their phone to create content and other daily reminders to post the content. Time of day and day of the week are less important at the beginning than getting it done. Similar to why your athlete attends practice for their sport, creating and posting content allows your athlete to get more reps in. The more reps they do, the better they get.

Also, the social media platforms provide feedback after each "rep," letting you know what content your audience resonates with. I'm not saying only post what other people like, but I am saying it's helpful to know when you talk about a topic that resonates with others and allows them to connect with you.

Consistency and volume are key.

The Importance of Engagement

The last key is having your athlete engage with their community. The best way to initiate this is by responding to comments.

At the beginning of this chapter, I pointed out how companies analyze engagement to determine which athletes might be best to partner with. Building a brand as a student-athlete involves active community engagement. Encourage your athlete to engage with fans, supporters, and followers both online and offline. For example, responding to a comment shows genuine appreciation for the time people spend looking at your athlete's content. It also makes their audience feel connected. When your athlete builds a community around their personal brand, they create a network of support and loyalty that will respond to products and collaborations they eventually present.

> **Tip**: *If your athlete's page is private, change it to public. Having a private page is like saying you're a store that has amazing products that people can purchase, but you're closed all the time. Eventually they won't come by anymore. People have even less patience when they are scrolling on social media. You want people and brands to see how amazing you are.*

PAY IT FORWARD

It's been tested and proven that people who help others without expectation of help in return lead a more fulfilled life. I'm sure you remember a time where someone looked out for you and how appreciative you were. I'd like to offer you the opportunity to create that same feeling of appreciation in someone else. To have this happen, I have an easy question for you.

Would you help someone you've never met if it didn't cost you any money and you knew it could change their financial situation for the better? If your answer is yes, I have a small request on behalf of that person. You probably won't meet them, but they are like you.

They are a parent who wants to offer their athlete the best opportunity they can to achieve their goals and follow their dreams. They also would love support along the way. This is where you come in.

The only way for me to achieve my goal of closing the financial and career gap for student-athletes is if first, I reach them. And since most people make their decision based on first impression (and reviews), if you have found this book helpful so far, would you please take 60 seconds or less right now and leave your review of this book by scanning the QR code below?

Your review will help

- More parents learn how to better support their athlete.

- More student-athletes pay for college.

- More families have financial freedom.

- Change people's lives for the better.

3 IDENTIFYING THE TARGET AUDIENCE

Now that you know your athlete's brand and they've started creating and posting content about it consistently, it's time to take the next step in brand building: identifying your athlete's audience.

Interests and Demographics

Knowing the interests and demographics of your athlete's audience is important for two reasons: content creation and pitching to companies.

Thoughtful content creation is key. By tailoring their content to the preferences and characteristics of their audience, your athlete increases their chances of engagement. Engagement then increases their reach and creates a loyal fan base. Remember, engagement is one of the most important elements for a brand. And it's the audience stickiness companies love to pay for.

To determine the audience's interest, look at analytics information on the social media account dashboard.The analytics will clarify what content performs well. Use this information to brainstorm more content around this topic or in this style.

If analytics information isn't available, look at who is leaving comments and which content receives the most engagement. Consider likes and views. Again, the more you and your athlete understand their audience, the more you are able to deliver valuable and relevant content, leading to higher levels of interaction, shares, and overall success. This does not mean continuously reposting content that got the highest views. It means looking at what resonates with the audience to find fresh new ways to share what they will love.

> *Tip*: Have your athlete check if their profile is registered as a pro, creator or business account (depending on the platform) so they can see their analytics.

Analytics will also show you demographic information. You can see the gender that favors your athlete's content and the age group their content resonates with. Use this information to fine-tune how your athlete addresses their audience or what they include in captions. An example of how this looks on TikTok and Instagram is below.

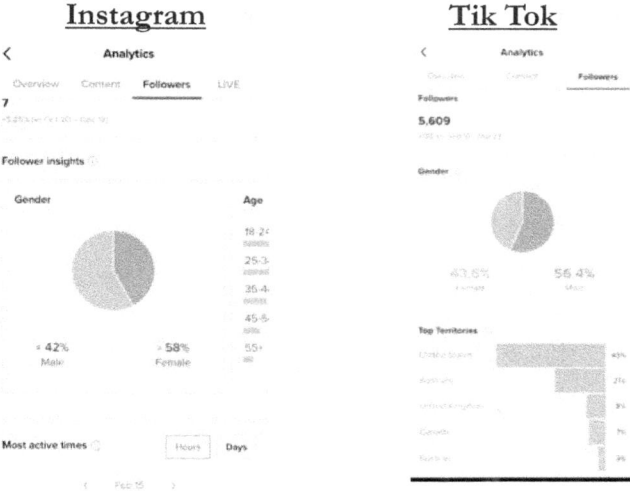

In addition, tracking engagement metrics is the foundation of being able to provide facts to let a company know why they'd benefit from partnering with your athlete as opposed to another social media influencer. Engagement is the holy grail of metrics. Even if there is an athlete with more followers than yours, a company will still want to work with yours if their engagement is high and their audience is actually a community. (Note: local brand deals are less about engagement, and we'll cover how to get those in a later chapter. This chapter will focus on what's needed for brand deals that are not local.)

The views, likes, shares, and comments in the analytics on a platform will convey your athlete's current engagement. Sometimes a platform will automatically combine these interactions into a statistic called engagement. Other platforms will list the interactions separately, and you will need to combine them yourself before calculating the engagement rate. The basic formula I use to determine engagement is below.

$$\text{Engagement Rate} = \frac{\text{Followers}}{\text{Likes (or all interactions)}} \times 100$$

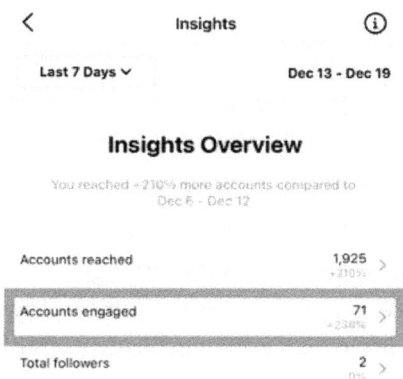

Insights Overview

You reached +210% more accounts compared to Dec 6 - Dec 12

Accounts reached	1,925 > +210%
Accounts engaged	71 > +238%
Total followers	2 > 0%

Using the analytics from the example page above, this account's overall engagement activity is 71, and they have 2 followers. This means their engagement rate is 2.8%.

The average engagement rate of a social media persona landing brand deals is about 4%. If your athlete's engagement isn't that high, don't worry. There are ways to improve engagement and there are offline ways to capitalize from NIL that don't take your athlete's engagement into account.

Identifying potential sponsors and partners

When you have a clear understanding of your athlete's audience demographics and interests, you can identify potential brand partnerships and collaborations that align with their followers' preferences. Companies are more likely to approach athletes whose audience matches their target market.

Observe who sponsors the posts and videos of other creators in your *AND Formula* niche, not just who sponsors athletes. Take note of the collaboration style. Did the creator read ad copy on a podcast? Was there a graphic shown about the sponsoring company? Was the company's product fully incorporated in the content? Analyzing this can give you a hint about what type of collaboration the company looks for.

Identifying the right sponsors and partners is crucial for a successful brand deal. Conduct thorough research to identify companies, other brands, or local businesses that align with your *AND Formula* and athlete's target audience. Look for companies or other brands that have a natural connection to your athlete's content. Consider factors such as industry relevance, company image, and previous or existing partnerships with other influencers and athletes.

Going local is a great place to start. Better yet, going local is the best place to start. Consider restaurants, bakeries, dentist offices, HVAC companies, and car dealerships in your athlete's community. Look at whose logo is listed on the banner as a sponsor of the local high school team. Local companies love a hometown hero, and you don't need a huge social following or high engagement numbers to generate the attention and/or crowd they'd want in order to collaborate.

Working with companies is often a game of numbers. The more outreach you do, the more companies actually come back with a yes. To get started, make a list of ten local companies below. Then, make a list of ten companies you've seen on social media that both fit within your *AND Formula* and have the same audience as your athlete:

BRAND DEAL LIST

Local Companies	Companies on Social Media

Keep in mind, everything that glitters isn't gold. Check your state's league associations to see if any types of endorsements are prohibited. For example, many high school leagues prohibit the endorsement of gambling (these include sports gambling apps), firearms, alcohol, and prescription medications.

Understanding your athlete's fanbase is an integral part of their success. By leveraging online analytics tools, having them engage with their audience, employing social listening, and interacting in person, you can...

- Gather valuable insights to craft compelling content.

- Forge strong connections with fans.

- Better position your athlete for bigger and bigger brand deals.

4 DEVELOPING THE VALUE PROPOSITION

We discussed a lot of data in the previous chapter. That's because understanding your audience is crucial for identifying your Unique Selling Proposition (USP). Your athlete's USP is the statement that explains how they are different from competitors. It not only shows companies and other brands how they stand out from competitors, but it also helps your athlete double down on their strengths.

Now that your athlete is creating content consistently, use the 2-for-1 Method to figure out their USP. The 2-for-1 Method allows you to gain insights into the needs, preferences, and pain points of your athlete's target audience, all while boosting engagement along the way.

The 2-for-1 Method focuses on three things: comments, questions, and profiles.

> 1. **Respond to Comments**: Reading comments helps you see what piques the audience's interest. It is also important for your athlete to respond to comments. This creates a conversation between your athlete and the person that has come to their page. When the viewer engages in the conversation, they become more invested in your athlete's content, stick around for more, and are more responsive to your athlete's product recommendations.
>
> 2. **Ask the Audience Questions**: Have your athlete ask questions to those who comment on their post. They can also ask questions using the survey and polls feature on Instagram Stories. On TikTok posts, they can ask a question as the caption. Pay attention to the answers left by followers and viewers. This feedback highlights the problems your athlete's audience faces or gaps in the other content that's out there for them.

3. **Look at Profiles**: Look at the profiles of the users who comment and follow your athlete. This will reveal what they are interested in. Having your athlete comment on their followers' posts will reinforce their audience's stickiness as well.

Once you use the 2-for-1 Method, you and your athlete will start to see trends that answer questions like "What knowledge or insights do I possess that others don't?" and "What do people like communicating with me about?" This is the unmet need of your audience. This is your athlete's USP.

Your athlete's USP should convey who your athlete's audience is, how your athlete benefits that audience, and what problem your athlete solves for their audience. For example, if your *And Formula* includes an interest in snacks, your athlete's USP could be, "The funny food-critic for your everyday snacks."

Write Your Athlete's USP here:

_____

Now, for some controversy. I've seen advice on social media about how you should look at what your competitors are doing for content and to see how you can be unique. I don't agree with this. Why? There's only one you. That's what makes you unique. A competitor can, at best, show you what has worked for them in the past for their audience, an audience that may not have the same interests as yours. At worst, a competitor might make you feel you haven't created enough content or accomplished enough brand deals.

Focus on your athlete's audience. It's your athlete's audience, not your athlete's competitors, who create your athlete's engagement and better position them for brand deals. *Back to business.*

Your athlete has probably been timed, measured, or assessed in some way for their sport. You may have even helped your athlete create an athletic resume. A company also wants to know how your athlete has helped other brands in the past, or at least what your athlete can reasonably guarantee for that specific company's brand in the future. To portray this, you should create a one-sheet (also called a rate card).

Not every company you want your athlete to work with will request a one-sheet, especially if they're local, but it's a great exercise to complete to make sure you and your athlete know your business. That way, when the time comes, you can talk to bigger companies about what your athlete brings to the table or directly send the company the one-sheet, if requested.

Your athlete's one-sheet should include at least three key pieces of information: a profile of your athlete's audience, audience statistics, and usage rights.

1. **Audience profile**: Include your athlete's audience demographics and their interests. Companies want to see whether your athlete's audience and their target audience are a match so they can gauge the return on the dollars they would spend on your athlete's endorsement.

2. **Audience Statistics and Engagement**: List your athlete's follower count, reach, and engagement rate on the platforms where they would post the sponsored content. You don't have to list this information for every platform. Also, if their follower count is extremely low, you can just list reach and engagement.

3. **Usage Rights**: This information lets a company know if your athlete requires an additional fee to exclusively promote the company's product or service. It also explains

your athlete's requirement(s) for a company to take content they create and use it as paid advertisement to drive customers to the company's website. You don't have to include a fee for these items on the one-sheet, but it is good for you to list these items so companies understand they are separate, additional benefits.

Initially, you can list your rates on a separate sheet that can be sent to companies after they are interested. (Unless they make you an offer before you even have the chance!)

> **Tip**: After your athlete's first brand deal, you can expand their one-sheet into a media toolkit with examples of how they visually drive campaigns. This is another way to set your athlete apart from other content creators a brand might be considering and show that your athlete is the best investment.

Aligning with Relevant Causes

So far, we've talked about packaging your athlete's brand for for-profit companies. Yet aligning their brand with relevant causes can be a powerful way to engage their audience, make a positive impact, and enhance their brand's reputation. There are many nonprofit organizations who would love to benefit from the partnership of a student-athlete. Here are some easy steps you can take to align your athlete's brand with causes.

Determine the causes and issues that are personally important to them. Reach out to organizations that are working on the causes they care about. Remember, collaborating with reputable and established organizations can lend credibility to your athlete's brand.

Explore potential partnership opportunities where your athlete can support initiatives or raise awareness for campaigns. You can also use the donation feature on their Instagram and TikTok page to directly bring awareness and funding to organizations they care about.

Instagram	TikTok
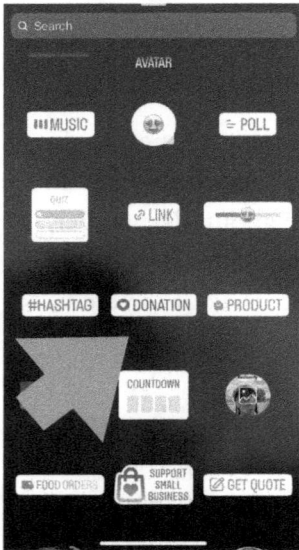	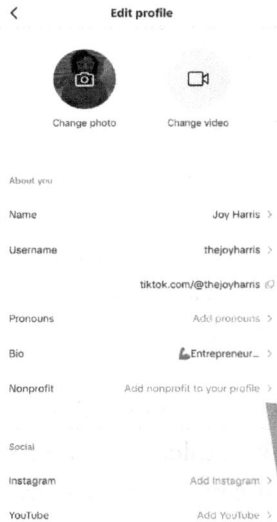

Lastly, partnering with non-profit organizations that are related to your athlete's sport can demonstrate their commitment to social responsibility and create revenue-generating opportunities for sponsorships or endorsements from organizations supporting similar causes. For example, volleyball player Lexi Sun's NIL deal with an apparel company came with the agreement that some of the proceeds would go to a sports psychology nonprofit she already championed.

5 APPROACHING POTENTIAL SPONSORS

If you're new to creating a brand, companies probably aren't flooding your DMs with deals. Not to worry, you don't have to wait for them to stumble across one of your athlete's social media handles. You can go to them.

In this chapter, I'll break down different types of brand partnerships. You'll also get a run down on the ones that take less than an hour to secure as opposed to the ones that require a lot more leverage but could result in more pay.

Low Hanging Fruit

Both Affiliate Programs and Marketplaces are great places to start in brand deal land. If you've ever heard your favorite YouTuber say "click the link in the description" or your favorite Instagrammer say "Use my code for a discount," that's an affiliate program.

An affiliate program allows individuals to sell products or services on behalf of a company in exchange for commission on each sell. So, when a person clicks the link and purchases something using the YouTuber's code, that YouTuber gets paid.

Affiliate programs aren't just limited to YouTubers and YouTube. There are a ton of companies that have affiliate programs and want to work with student-athletes. There are sports-related companies that range from apparel, like No Bull, to ticketing, like SeatGeek. There are also companies outside of sports like Hubspot and Fiverr that pay up to $100 per transaction when people purchase. Think about it: an audience with high engagement could result in your student-athlete earning $100 per hour. Not a bad gig compared to the retail or fast-food job you were squeezing in at their age.

Keep in mind, each affiliate program has its own payout amount. But becoming a brand partner is easy. Oftentimes, it's as simple as scrolling to the bottom of a company's website, clicking the link that says Partner

Program, and filling out the short application. It's a process that usually takes 30 minutes or less, but your athlete can get paid from it over and over again as long as their audience clicks the link and makes a purchase.

Marketplaces like Mogl and Dreamfield Sports also make it easy for student-athletes to get brand deals. A marketplace is a company that uses software to connect businesses to individuals who can provide them with a service they need. Businesses come to marketplaces because they have options at scale, and individuals sign up for marketplaces because it gets you in front of opportunities you wouldn't otherwise have access to. The marketplace usually takes a fee for making the connection and then passes payment from the business on to the individual.

To join these marketplaces, it's as simple as completing an application. Once accepted, your athlete can review the company's opportunities that are available, decide which ones to endorse, and agree to create awareness for the companies they like.

> *Tip*: Each brand usually has a deliverable. This is content they want created, posted, and/or submitted by a certain deadline, so make sure you read the requirements of the collaboration.

Landing Local

Local businesses have deep roots in the communities they serve. And the people who own them often root for others in their community to do well, especially if it leads to a positive community impact. This makes local businesses a perfect place to start for brand deals. Not only does it benefit the business owner and the community they pay taxes in, your athlete has a better chance at a successful partnership response rate because they are already known by people in the area such as teammates, relatives, and church members who will support simply because you asked them to.

Like affiliates and marketplaces, you will need to take the first step to make these deals happen. Call or stop by to talk to the business owner about how your athlete can drive more customers to their business. Think outside the box for this one. Posting a picture on social media is great, but can your athlete offer to bring in a certain number of customers on the business's slowest night? Or perhaps calling each of the customers on the businesses mailing list to leave a special message about an upcoming promotion? Can they produce a creative video that shows them testing out the businesses best item in-store? This may seem like heavy lifting at first, but knocking this local deal out the park not only gets your athlete's feet wet, but gives them leverage for the next...bigger...brand deal.

In addition, attending local events, engaging with community leaders, and building relationships with local business owners can lead to brand partnership opportunities.

National Companies

Oftentimes, larger companies want to see both engagement and previous brand collaborations from your athlete. These types of companies tend to reach out to the athletes and influencers they are interested in, but that doesn't mean you can't get on their radar and initiate the conversation so your athlete is considered.

First look for companies and other brands that align with your athlete's target audience. Study their products, services, marketing campaigns, and past brand deals to understand their goals and values. Then, with this refined list, proceed in initiating the conversation.

There are two ways to initiate the conversation. One, you can work with your athlete to create a sample series. Instead of waiting on the company collaboration, encourage your athlete to start creating content about the companies they love. Reviews, GRWM (get ready with me), and taste tests are great ways to show off products your athlete is into. This demonstrates their authenticity around the product and shows your athlete can create engaging content that their audience responds to (which companies love).

Two, reach out to the brand. You should be able to grab a general contact email or phone number off their website or social media. Draft an email that inquires about the best point of contact for collaborations. Once you're in touch with the correct person, submit your pitch in the way they request.

> *Tip*: Food and beverage brands list their website and consumer contact number on the back of their products.

Don't overlook smaller or emerging companies. They may have larger budgets for student-athletes. Collaborating with them can be mutually beneficial as they often offer more creative freedom and may be open to long-term partnerships as they grow.

SCAN ME TO ACCESS TEMPLATE EMAIL
YOU CAN SEND TO COMPANIES

What to Pitch

Local businesses tend to be less prescriptive in what they'd want your athlete to do; however, larger companies tend to have a specific type of collaboration in mind. Below is a list of options to have in your arsenal:

- **Sponsored Content**: This is the most traditional and widely recognized form of brand collaboration. In a sponsored content collaboration, the athlete creates content that promotes a company's product, service, or campaign and discloses their partnership with the company. This can take the form of social media posts, blog articles, videos, or product reviews.

- **Ambassadorships**: An ambassadorship is a long-term collaboration where the athlete serves as a brand ambassador. As an ambassador, the athlete represents the company over an extended period, promoting its products or services consistently. This type of collaboration typically involves a higher level of commitment and involvement from both the athlete and the company.

- **Giveaways and Contests**: Companies often collaborate with athletes to run giveaways or contests, where the athlete promotes the opportunity for their followers to win products or experiences provided by the company. Giveaways and contests can help generate buzz, engagement, and company awareness.

- **Event Hosting or Attendance**: Companies may invite athletes to attend events or host autograph signings. These events can range from meet-and-greets to product launches. The athlete contributes to the event's promotion and coverage, leveraging their presence and reach to generate excitement and engage the target audience.

- **Content Creation**: Companies may collaborate with an athlete by asking the athlete to create content that matches the company's brand and marketing efforts. This could involve the athlete developing marketing materials such as content for the company's social media channels. In this type of collaboration, the athlete's expertise and creative skills are utilized to enhance the company's content strategy.

- **Takeovers**: Companies occasionally allow athletes to take over their social media accounts for a specific period. During the takeover, the athlete shares content directly with the company's audience, providing a fresh perspective and engaging the followers in a new and exciting way.

The list above is not exhaustive, and your athlete does not have to pursue every type of collaboration. One of the keys to a successful collaboration is knowing your athlete's strengths—and then choosing formats that play to their personality.

Knowing Your Pitch

Regardless of what your offer is, your athlete knowing their pitch—and knowing that it starts when they first present themselves—is the most important element. The pitch starts with the first email or phone call. You're not going to read their entire one-sheet on the first call, but do have your facts together.

Compensation and Negotiation

There is no standard rate for brand deals. It varies based on the company and the value the athlete can deliver. For example, YouTube pays creators approximately $18.00 per thousand views while Tik Tok pays creators about $.04 per thousand views. Payment amount can change even more dramatically when it's a product or service company you're collaborating with. Recognize that compensation can vary widely based on factors such as your athlete's level of influence and the scope of the collaboration. To start, I recommend hearing what the company offers and then negotiating up by providing extra value. For example, you can offer additional content or exclusivity. Then, the higher, negotiated amount becomes the baseline for your athlete's next brand deal.

Thoroughly review the terms and conditions of any contract or agreement presented to you. Pay close attention to compensation structure, exclusivity clauses, contract duration, usage rights, and any additional obligations or restrictions. Understand what is expected of your athlete and ensure that the compensation offered aligns with the scope of the collaboration.

Don't be afraid to negotiate for fair and equitable terms. Consider factors such as the level of exclusivity, the time and effort required, and the value your athlete brings to the company's campaign. Articulate your athlete's value proposition and highlight any unique aspects that make your athlete stand out. Negotiate in a professional and respectful manner, keeping in mind that successful negotiations often involve compromise from both sides.

> **Tip**: *If you know your athlete is worth more, ask for it. You can't be afraid of the no. If you don't land the deal, adjust next time. They're not the only company in the world.*

6 COMPLIANCE AND REPORTING REQUIREMENTS

The NCAA no longer prohibits a student from using their name, image, and likeness for compensation. However, boosters and NIL entities cannot talk to recruits about enrolling at a school or offer deals based upon whether athletes select a particular school. Also, student-athletes cannot be paid based on how they perform while playing their sport. No matter how many people and organizations you hear cross the line in the space, remember it's not cool for your athlete to ask a coach, "How much NIL money can I get if I go here?"

The NCAA has stated that student-athletes must follow state law surrounding NIL, and if no state law is in place, they can participate in NIL activities.

Schools and conferences can impose reporting requirements; however, it is not explicitly stated whether schools and conferences can impose additional NIL-related restrictions.

State laws vary from state-to-state, but some common provisions include:

- Prohibiting schools from withholding scholarships or eligibility to participate in athletics from athletes who exercise NIL rights

- Prohibiting schools from providing NIL compensation to current or prospective student-athletes or using NIL agreements as recruiting inducements

- Allowing student-athletes to hire agents, attorneys, or other representatives to assist them with NIL contracts, and providing requirements for these representatives

- Requiring athletes to disclose NIL agreements to schools, and prohibiting agreements that conflict with school or team contracts

- Prohibiting athletes from endorsing alcohol, tobacco, marijuana, gambling, adult entertainment, or other morally questionable activities

- Protecting the intellectual property rights of schools

- Requiring schools to provide financial literacy training for athletes

- Allowing schools to prohibit athletes from engaging in NIL activities during official team activities

Note that not every state requires each of the provisions above.

Many high school athletic associations have followed suit with the NCAA by restricting participation in endorsement-related activities while playing for a school or in school uniform. Similar to NCAA athletics, the high school level also tends to prohibit the endorsement of "risqué" activities such as gambling, alcohol, and prescription medications.

From my own discussions in the space, I often come across headlines and hearsay about what can and cannot be done in a state, but when I ask for the written regulations, the assumed policies are not listed. Make sure you ask for the **official written policy** of your state, school or conference so you can both stay in compliance and participate in ALL the opportunities you are eligible for.

Due to guidelines required by student visas, most international students have not been able to participate in NIL thus far. There have been attempts to have international student-athletes included by adjusting visa status or limiting deals to those managed by third parties. This has not yet been widely adapted, and there has not yet been a statement at the NCAA level.

Schools are able to support NIL under the current NCAA policy via methods such as matching students to NIL resources, providing graphics and stock photos themselves, and offering financial literacy workshops. Each college and university is different in their level of support. However, it's important that you know what your athlete's school (or potential school) is doing to support NIL so your athlete can benefit from it.

SCAN ME FOR NCAA NIL POLICY

Get down to business

Earning money under NIL is a business. It is important for you and your athlete to establish a solid business structure as they engage in these entrepreneurial ventures. There are many YouTube videos and qualified business professionals that can help you gain valuable insights into the legal and financial aspects of your new business endeavor.

As you do your research, some things to consider include the type of business entity that's best for your athlete (e.g. sole proprietorship, partnership, or limited liability company), how to secure a federal employer identification number, the articles that need to be filed at your state's corporation commission, a business banking institution, and the payment processor you'd like to use to receive payments from companies. As you gain momentum, liability protection, tax implications, scalability, contract negotiation, and brand management are additional areas to learn and seek guidance in to ensure your athlete makes informed decisions and optimizes their NIL opportunities.

7 MAXIMIZING NIL OPPORTUNITIES

Right now, your athlete can earn income under NIL in more ways than just brand deals.

Social Media Platforms

Many platforms have a way for an influencer's audience to support them regardless of their follower count. Fanbase is a free social media app that allows anyone to receive a one-time payment, called love, or a subscription fee from their followers. Patreon allows users to build memberships that followers pay for to receive content access. Instagram has badges followers can use to send a one-time payment of any amount. These features allow the audience to send money directly to your athlete simply based on the content they create. Other platforms, like Youtube and their Adsense program, pay for the views or attention your athlete gains.

Collectives

A lot of the NIL deals that schools distribute to student-athletes are actually their collectives. A collective refers to an organized entity or program created alongside a college or university to provide resources, assistance, and infrastructure to student-athletes via NIL. In the simplest terms, an NIL collective is a program designed to facilitate athletes' potential endorsement opportunities. Each school can have its own NIL collective(s) or there may be several within one conference.

Because colleges and universities aren't allowed to provide student-athletes with NIL funds, alumni and boosters form the collectives. The alumni and boosters in the collective raise money to support athletes that currently attend or decide to attend the school without technically breaking NCAA policy. (Many of the headlines about an athlete going to a certain school and receiving $3 million dollars is because the collective is paying them.)

A collective can be structured like a nonprofit where the student gets paid to do charitable work.

Alternatively, a collective can operate like a business-matching organization, putting athletes in touch with businesses and then paying them to work with that business.

It is estimated that 92% of Power 5 schools have a collective. Some schools have collectives that have designated millions of dollars to support athletes, such as Ole Miss's the Grove Collective ($10 million) and Auburn's On to Victory Collective ($12 million). Other schools' collectives have doubled down on the perks athletes get, such as University of Oregon, which is heavily supported by the co-founder of Nike, Phil Knight.

It's important to note collectives are not just at the college level. Also, the structure and offerings of these collectives can vary from one school or university to another.

Determine if the school your athlete is at or wants to attend has a collective, familiarize yourself with what they have to offer, and encourage your athlete to connect with them. By leveraging the collective's support, student-athletes can unlock new revenue streams, enhance their personal brands, and capitalize on the unique platform that their university offers. This ultimately leads to increased earning potential under NIL.

Networking

Once your athlete gets a brand deal, cultivate strong relationships with the sponsoring company by encouraging your athlete to deliver on their promises and exceed expectations. Track and measure performance on sponsored posts so you know exactly what your athlete brings to the table. Encourage your athlete to consistently communicate, provide updates on campaign progress, and seek feedback. Long-term partnerships are often more valuable than one-time collaborations.

Strong, positive relationships with a sponsor company not only leads to repeat collaboration, but your athlete can also strategically leverage brand deals as networking opportunities to increase their chances of getting hired in positions at the companies they collaborate with. By establishing strong professional relationships with company representatives during brand deals, your athlete can showcase their skills, work ethic, and professionalism. This can leave a lasting impression on the company, potentially opening doors for future employment opportunities once their athletic career concludes.

Additionally, student-athletes can use these brand partnerships to learn valuable business insights from industry experts. By actively engaging with these experts, student-athletes can seek mentorship and gain knowledge about launching their own products or ventures in the future. This exposure to real-world business education can equip them with the necessary skills and guidance to navigate the entrepreneurial world successfully.

Entrepreneurship

Brand deals aren't the only way to build your athlete's nest egg. Remember, your athlete is a brand. Once they have built a community, they can launch their own products and merchandise or even license their brand.

There are different avenues for licensing and merchandising, such as apparel, accessories, collectibles, and digital products. There are also several companies that specialize in sports merchandise and licensing agreements. Research existing deals in your athlete's sport to understand the possibilities. And make sure you take the necessary steps to monitor and protect their brand.

Athletes like Bijan Robinson and Santia Deck are paving the way in parlaying brand deals into their own business ventures. Bijan launched his own mustard line, Bijan Mustardson, and Santia is the owner of the sneaker company Tronus. Entrepreneurship is no small feat, but with patience, guidance, practice, and education, it can create income without limits.

Your athlete can and should be successful before going pro. Your athlete can and should be successful whether they go pro or not. There are the naysayers who are married to the good ol' days, but those people aren't worth your attention. They aren't rooting for your athlete's success. I am.

We've covered a lot in this book. To summarize:

- It is possible for your athlete to make money RIGHT NOW, no matter the sport they play, what level they are at, or how many followers they have.

- Through consistently building brand, cultivating community, applying creativity, and taking initiative, you can help your athlete generate money to pay for their own everyday expenses, cover tuition so when they graduate both of you are debt-free, and create a nest egg to fund their future dreams.

- Though this book is written for you, you can teach all the information to your athlete.

I hope this book makes it easier for you to help your athlete accomplish their financial goals. I appreciate your purchase and your attention. I do not take it for granted. And it's because of your support that I am able to support so many other families and student-athletes on their journey.

Thank you,

P.S. Would you be opposed to setting up your athlete for success a little faster?

SCAN TO HOP IN A PERSONAL SESSION

<u>WITH ME</u>

ABOUT THE AUTHOR

Joy Harris is a successful entrepreneur with over 10+ years of experience helping others scale their ambitions. She is passionate about student-athlete success and helping families gain the leverage necessary for them to win on-and-off the field. Joy is a prolific speaker and author of The Student Guide to NIL and Singing Ain't Enough.

www.ingramcontent.com/pod-product-compliance
Lightning Source LLC
Chambersburg PA
CBHW070945210326
41520CB00021B/7066